The Dynamic Art of
BREAKING

The Dynamic Art of BREAKING

by

Pu Gill Gwon

Printed in the United States of America
Library of Congress Catalog Card Number: 77-89191

Eleventh Printing 1984

ISBN-0-89750-023-7

OHARA PUBLICATIONS, INCORPORATED
BURBANK, CALIFORNIA

Dedication

I dedicate this book to my wife, Bokhee, and to my children, especially Yise, my elder son, and Seung Chul, my second son; and to my daughters, Jung Shin and Seung Shin.

publishers note

We must take this opportunity to caution the reader to exercise great care while practicing the techniques described in this book. The methods described and illustrated are based upon years of practical experience. But injuries can still occur. Often injuries come through exceeding the recommended schedule, failure to go through the long, toughening phase, human error or carelessness. Make this a serious study, not a game.

We recommend that the reader study the correct way to hold and strike targets in all techniques. Observe the all-important toughening techniques. Avoid breaking hard things with soft hands.

Pace yourself according to your progress. Do not exceed the recommended training schedule. Scar tissue can form too quickly, trapping the tendons and causing great pain. (The scar tissue builds up around the tendons, reducing their elasticity, flexibility and function.) Be patient. Be cautious. Make sure that you use only the striking areas called for in each technique. For example, in a fist strike, use only the knuckles of the index and second finger. These are stronger, structurally, than the other two fingers. To use the third and fourth fingers, or only one of the large knuckles, is to invite injury. The same principle applies to all other striking areas and techniques.

By all means, if you have questions regarding the safety of any technique, or if you experience continuing pain after performing a technique, *see your physician without delay!*

About the Author

Pu Gill Gwon was born near Seoul, Korea. When he was a youngster he went with his family to live in Pusan, Korea.

In his schooling there he learned boxing—Western style. For young Pu Gill Gwon, his work in the boxing ring set him on the road to martial arts success. He won the Junior Boxing Championships in his tournament class.

In 1954, he met his first Korean martial arts master, Ha Dae Young, and began the study of tae kwon do. From there, he began to branch out into the study of yudo, with Chang Hang Je. When he had completed high school, he continued his studies in tae kwon do, specializing in ji do kwan, a special style, utilizing many techniques of self-defense.

In 1958, Pu Gill Gwon joined the Korean Navy's Underwater Demolition Team. His superb physique, excellent health and agility, developed through a religiously dedicated pursuit of the martial arts, saw him through the difficult training so well that he jumped from student to instructor and was assigned to the Korean Naval Intelligence section. Mr. Gwon regards his tours as a teacher and in the Intelligence division as probably the most hazardous of his life.

In 1964, Pu Gill Gwon started teaching yudo. The branch he taught is Kyung Ki Do yudo, an especially popular branch of Korean yudo. Two years later, Pu Gill Gwon was named Director of the Kyung Ki Do Yudo Association. In 1967, he joined the International Tae Kwon Do Federation.

Pu Gill Gwon visited the United States in 1971 to demonstrate his techniques, including his dynamic breaking methods, at various martial arts expositions. The public response was enthusiastic. He stayed on and opened his first dojang in Baltimore, Maryland. Today Pu Gill Gwon has eight schools in various locations around the United States. He attributes the popularity of his classes to the dedication the students have once they get underway. The art of dynamic breaking, as developed by Pu Gill Gwon, has brought about standing ovations across the country. This began in 1975 at the Martial Arts Exposition in Chicago promoted by Jimm Jones.

In this book, Pu Gill Gwon shares his dynamic art of breaking techniques with the seriously practicing advanced tae kwon do student and all martial artists intent on expanding their arsenal of techniques. These are the same as those Mr. Gwon demonstrated in Chicago at the MaComer Convention Center in 1975. These techniques carried Pu Gill Gwon through countless self-defense situations and earned him fame in this country as a martial arts superstar.

Forward

In the martial arts, breaking techniques are not goals in themselves. They must be part of the total study of the martial arts. They are for the advanced student. They are the means whereby you will perfect your mastery of the martial art. Breaking techniques produce more accuracy and control than does sparring. Power, too, comes through the perfection of breaking techniques. Sparring is fine up to a point, but I maintain that breaking is more difficult.

Accuracy, speed and power are the essential elements of breaking techniques. I speak of practice of the martial arts. It is a general statement. One can only speak of breaking techniques in specific terms.

In breaking techniques, your use of accuracy must be exact; your aim must go for the target and be totally accurate. Properly done, you will know just how effective your strikes are. You know that if the target had been a point on an opponent's body, you would have shattered it. Breaking techniques develop confidence. Unless you are full contact at full power and without protective equipment—a practice I do not recommend—you can never really know how effective your strikes are in sparring.

Yet weight is not the only factor. No matter how hard you hit something, it will not be damaged if it moves with the power of your punch. But if your punch moves faster than the target bounces away from it, the target has no choice but to break. This is demonstrated in the chapter on "Speed Breaking." The "Speed

Practice" chapter shows how to develop your own individual speed.

It would be foolish to kick an opponent in the thigh and expect his knee to break.

You have to focus your strike exactly on the pressure point. In breaking you have the opportunity and the obligation to strike an exact spot. After your partner learns "How To Hold A Board," you must learn "Where To Strike A Target." If you don't hit the right spot on your target, you will be very aware of it. It simply will not break. Practice "Control Kicking." It will help you develop focus. The words in quotes are the titles of chapters in this book. Use them as a guide. And practice, practice, practice.

In many television dramas, actors pretend to break something by striking at it, and then cocking their fists in something of a swatting motion. In reality, this does not work. Again, some people believe that you should aim for the surface of your target. All materials have flexibility, some more than others. Bricks bend very little; wood and bones have a great deal of flexibility. Oddly enough, it is these materials which have the *most* bend to them that are the hardest to break. Everything breaks only after it is pushed past the limit of how far it bends. You must have the power and speed to push it past that limit before it has a chance to recover. You must aim for "Penetration."

You can have weight and speed behind your strikes, but without concentration you will have neither focus nor penetration. If your mind is elsewhere, your concentration wanders and your worries about injury swim into your thoughts, and you cannot fix your mind on your target. Concern yourself only with the project at hand. That is a good practice for everything, especially the martial arts. Put your whole mind to what you are doing at the moment, and you will accomplish what you start out to do. Sound philosophy and meditation for everything, as well as the martial arts.

Good breaking technique demands daily practice, concentrated focus, confidence and ability. You must have a good physique and you must have many martial arts skills. Then you will find that power, accuracy and speed are your best elements in the development of expert breaking techniques.

Pu Gill Gwon

Contents

4

3

5

2

1

How To Practice

The proper way to learn each of the techniques demonstrated in this book is to practice one step at a time. You want to master the first movement before going on to the second move. You want to master the first two movements before going on to the third move, and so on.

When learning how to break from the right forward stance, for example, you should first practice swinging your left foot forward, spinning on your right foot (photo 1). Practice that movement one hundred times. When you have that move mastered, practice move 1 and move 2 together one hundred times, spinning on your left foot and bringing your right foot around backward (photo 2). Next, add the third part of the technique, jumping and breaking the target with a ridgefoot (photos 3,4,5). Practice move 1, move 2 and move 3 together one hundred times. Then you will have mastered the entire technique.

Although the number of repetitions suggested is one hundred for each part and each combination, the point is to master it before you go on to the next step. If you can really master it in fifty repetitions, that is fine. If it takes two hundred repetitions before you are happy with it, then by all means do two hundred. For a technique to be successful, each part must be done correctly.

Chapter 1

STRIKING AREAS

Each technique uses a specific part of the body to make the strike. The following photos illustrate the exact portion which makes contact upon impact.

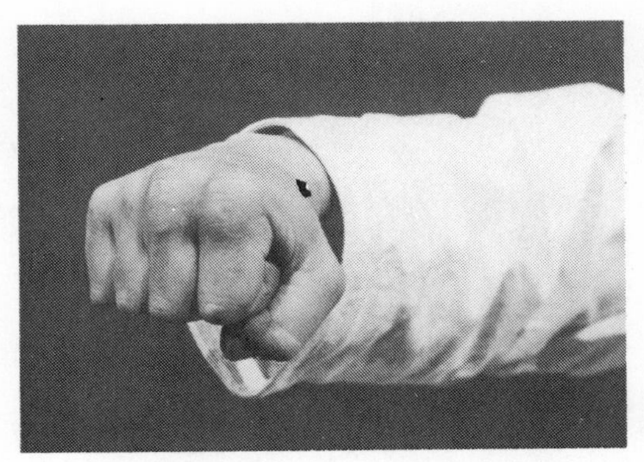

FIST—use the front part of the first knuckle of your index and second fingers.

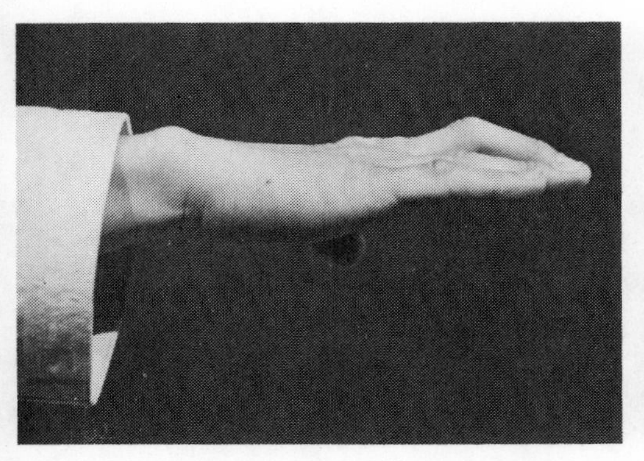

KNIFE HAND—use the outside edge of your hand below the first knuckle.

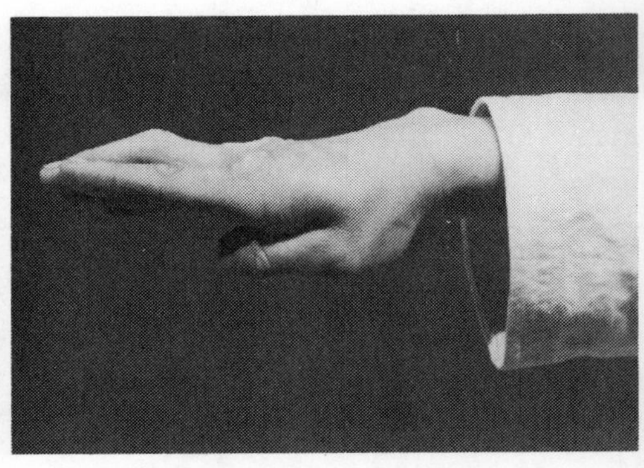

RIDGEHAND—use the inside edge of your hand above the base of the thumb.

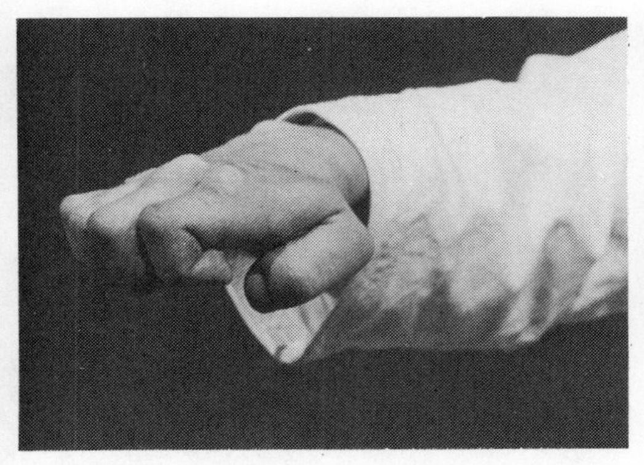

JOINT FINGER—use the front part of the second knuckle of your index and second fingers.

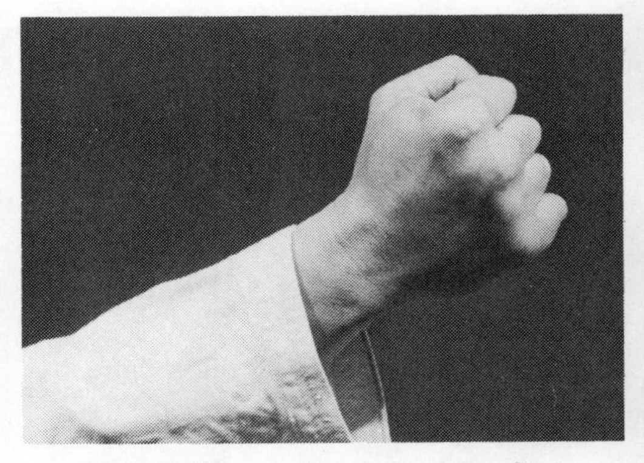

BACKFIST—use the top of the first knuckle of your index and second fingers.

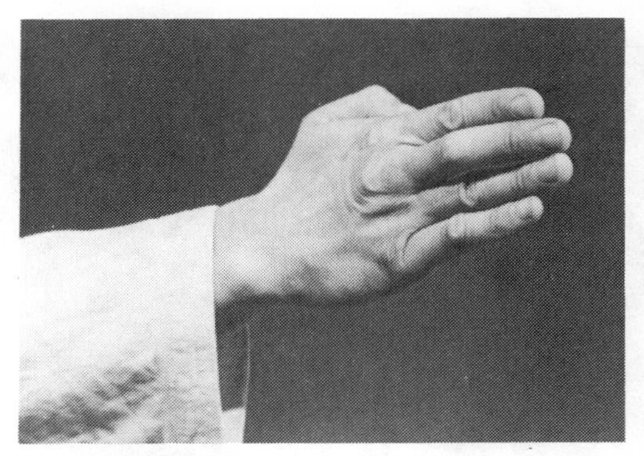
FINGERTIP—use the tips of your middle fingers.

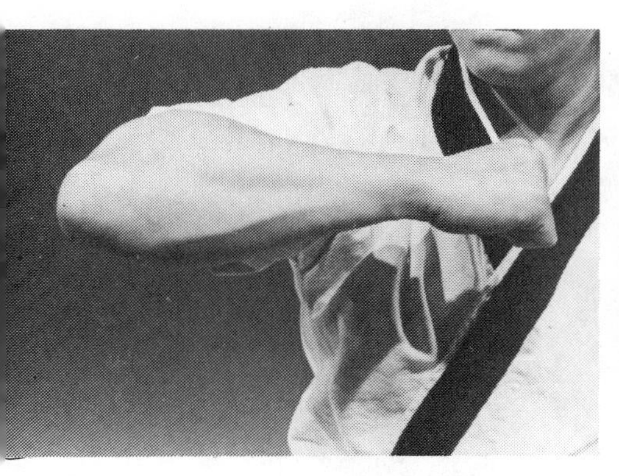
ELBOW—use the forepart of your elbow.

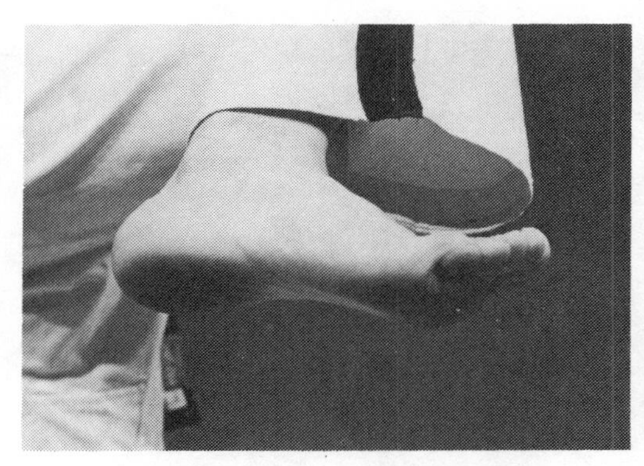
RIDGE FOOT—use the middle of the outside edge of your foot.

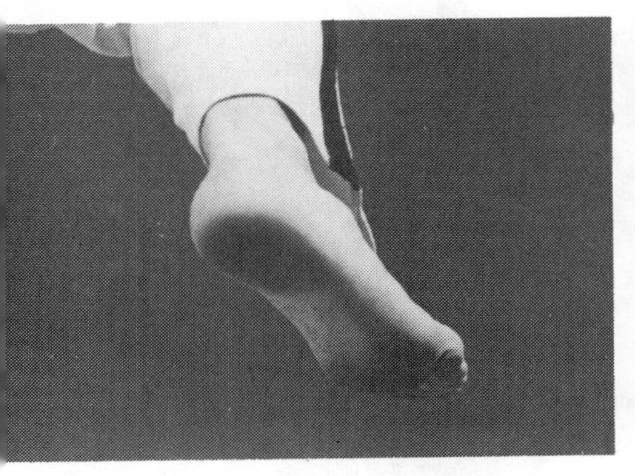
HEEL—use the edge of the ball of your heel.

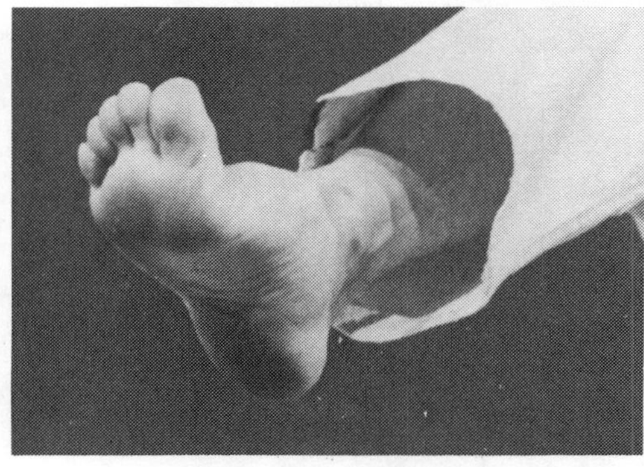
BALL FOOT—use the front part of the ball of your foot.

Chapter 2

PRACTICE BOARDS

The purpose of practice boards is to harden the areas of the body used to strike and break. The best schedule is to strike 20 times with each striking area of each hand and each foot. This should be done every two to three hours throughout the day, every day. If you do not have that much time to train, strike 40 times with each area of each hand and foot during one session every day.

If you practice more than the recommended schedule on any one day, your hands and feet will become too sore to practice the next day. Since you will get maximum benefits from practicing every day, it is best not to do too much in any one day.

UPRIGHT PRACTICE BOARD

The upright practice board is a board on a stand which presents one target at shoulder level and another at knee level. The targets are wrapped with material to keep you from injuring your hand or foot. The board is tied to a base so that it can swing with the impact. This is the first practice board for students.

Toughening the Fist

(1) Bring your fist straight back. (2) Move your body weight forward along with your fist and (3) strike,

using your body weight to add to the force of your fist. (4) Bring your fist straight back and repeat exercise.

Toughening the Knife Hand

(1) Angle your body 90 degrees to the practice board. (2) Swing the top of your body and (3) strike with full force. (A) Close-up of knife hand strike position. (B) For ridgehand, turn hand over.

A

2

3

B

Toughening the Ball of the Foot (A)

(1) From the ready stance, (2) lift up your knee, the higher the better, and (3) kick straight out with the ball of your foot—use full force.

1

Toughening the Ball of the Foot (B)

(1) Take a ready stance to the far left of the upright practice board. (2) Swing your leg up in a roundhouse kick and (3) make full-force contact. This strengthens the ball of the foot from a different direction.

1

2

3

2

3

1

Toughening the Heel

(1) Take a ready stance at a 90-degree angle to the upright board. (2) Bend your knee up as high as

2

possible and (3) strike as hard as possible with your heel. (4) Take a ready stance and repeat exercise.

HAND-HELD PRACTICE BOARDS

FLAT BOARD

The flat and round practice boards are not wrapped and are for advanced students. They rely on grooves cut all the way through the board and running half the length or more. These grooves allow the force of the impact to be absorbed slightly as the wood bends through the small space of the groove and hits the other side. The flat practice board is used to toughen the entire striking area used in a technique; the round board presents a single-point target for concentrated toughening of a spot of the striking area. Always strike the boards hard enough to hear a cracking noise as one side of the wood hits the other side.

Toughening the Knife Hand

(1) As with the round board, sit and (2) bring the weight of your body down with your hand, (3) striking the board with all of the striking area of the knife hand.

Toughening the Fist

(1) Kneel directly above the flat board, holding it with your nonstriking hand. (2) Bring your shoulder and weight down, giving extra force to your blow and (3) hit with the full striking area of the fist.

Toughening the Heel

With your foot raised and your knee bent, hold the flat practice board (1) with the hand on the same side of your body and (2) bring it down hard on your heel. (3) Make sure it is hard enough for you to hear a cracking sound from the board.

Toughening the Ball of the Foot

(1) With the flat board in the hand opposite the foot you want to toughen, raise your foot and (2) bring down the board on the ball of your outstretched foot.

2

3

2

3

ROUND BOARD

Toughening the Knife Hand

(1) In a sitting position, raise hand over your head and (2) bring the weight of your body down with your hand, (3) striking the board full-force with a point of the striking area of your hand.

1

The Sand Box

To toughen your fingertips, use a small box about one foot high, filled nearly full of sand.

(1) Stand directly over the sandbox and (2) move your body with the downward strike of your fingertips, putting more force into your blow. (3) Do this as fast as you can, because it also develops speed.

2

3

Chapter 3

SPEED BREAKING

There are three steps to breaking. First, you must toughen your hand or foot. Second, you must develop enough speed to go through the object before it is hit out of the way. If you do not have enough speed, you will simply knock it over. (Also, you must hit with the hardest part of your hand or foot, or the flesh will cushion your blow.) Only when you have mastered the first two steps, are you ready for the third step—actually breaking a target.

Bottle Breaking

(1) You are going to break a bottle at the neck. Get into ready position in front of it, kneeling on one knee. (2) Bring your hand back across your body. (3) As you strike with a knife hand, twist your body around with it to give you more power. Build up speed. (4) Hit the

bottle with the top, bony part of the knife hand as the striking area. If you hit it fast enough, it will break cleanly at the neck.

CAUTION: Do not attempt bottle breaking until you have mastered the art of speed breaking on less dangerous objects.

Speed Breaking with Jumping Roundhouse Kick

(1) From ready position, (2) crouch for your jump. As you jump (3) push your nonkicking knee up as far as possible. (4) Switch knees in air, bringing up your kicking

knee. (5) Finally, twist your body as you kick.

The application for this technique is shown here (A) in a jumping roundhouse kick to the opponent's face.

A

Chapter 4

SPEED PRACTICE

It is important that you always practice your techniques at full speed and that you try to improve your speed. Practicing with a tree branch will help you develop speed. The branches of a young green tree will bend and leaves will remain on the branch if you strike slowly. If you are fast enough, the leaves will fall.

For the best results, speed practice each of your techniques 10 times every two to three hours, throughout the day—every day. If your schedule will not allow you that much time, practice each set of 10 repetitions twice daily. Once in the morning and once in the evening would be good.

Knife Hand Speed Practice

(1) Twist your body with ready knife hand. (2) Strike at the leaves as hard and as fast as possible. (3) After making contact, follow through.

Fist Speed Practice

(1) From the ready position, (2) strike as hard and as fast as possible. (3) The leaves will drop only if you are fast enough.

2

3

2

3

High Side Kick Speed Practice

(1) From a ready stance, (2) bend your knee up (3) as high as you can and (4) snap the kick out, then (5) to the side and down, in one fluid motion, bending your knee.

2

4

5

Roundhouse Kick Speed Practice

(1) Take a ready stance a little back from the tree. (2) Lift your knee as your body turns and (3) *lift the heel* of the foot you are standing on when your

other foot makes contact. You will gain more power as your body weight is added to the force of your kick. (4) Take a ready stance and repeat exercise.

Speed Practice with a Magazine

You can use a magazine in place of a tree branch. (1) Take the ready posi-

tion, (2) bring your knee up and (3) kick in an arc; up, then (4) down.

Chapter 5

HOW TO HOLD A BOARD

To perform breaking techniques effectively and safely—for both you and your partners—all participants must learn how to hold the target board correctly. The basic rule is to always hold the board with your knuckles parallel to the grain of the wood, not perpendicular to it.

Here a student shows how to hold a board in each hand. The fingers are in the front and the thumbs at the back. Notice he is holding them on the side. DO NOT HOLD THE ENDS OF THE GRAIN. Hold the board with the grain parallel to the tips of your fingers.

¾ VIEW

Two people holding a board. Their outside feet are in front, and their inside feet are in back. Their shoulders are together, and each hand holds a corner, outside hand on the bottom and inside hand on top.

Chapter 6

WHERE TO STRIKE A TARGET

To break boards successfully, you must know where to hit them. You must also strike *with* the grain, never against it. Generally speaking, most strikes are to the middle part of the end of the board, with the grain parallel to the direction of the strike.

Fist Strike Breaking

Hit the board in the middle of the bottom part of the board. Make sure the grain runs up and down, vertically.

Knife Hand Breaking

Hit the board on the middle of one side. The grain runs across, horizontally.

Fingertip Breaking

If you strike with your hand held vertically, make sure the grain is vertical. Hit the board in the middle at the top. (If you strike horizontally, the grain should be horizontal and you should strike at one of the ends.)

Elbow Breaking

Come across the board and strike in the middle of the right-hand end. The grain runs horizontally.

Ridgehand Breaking

Strike the middle of one end. Keep the grain horizontal.

Backfist Breaking

Hit the board on the end in the middle. The grain is horizontal.

Front Kick Breaking

With the ball of your foot, kick the board at the bottom in the middle. The grain should be vertical.

Roundhouse Breaking

Come across the board and kick the end in the middle. Make sure the grain is horizontal.

Sidekick Breaking

Kick the middle of the end of the board. Keep the grain running horizontally.

Hook Kick Breaking

With your heel, come across the board and break it at the end in the middle. Grain goes horizontally.

Spin Kick Breaking

Again, come across the board, kick it in the middle of one end. The grain is horizontal.

Turning Back Kick Breaking

Kick the middle end of the board, keeping the grain horizontal.

Chapter 7

PENETRATION

Always go beyond your target. Follow through. If you stop your strike at the surface of the target, you will not go through it. Strike deeply, and you will always break your target.

RIGHT

A deep strike—penetration

WRONG

Too shallow

WRONG
No follow through

RIGHT
Go past your target

WRONG
The sidekick stops too soon

RIGHT
Kick deeply—you will go through

Chapter 8

BREAKING TECHNIQUES

Breaking techniques are the heart of this book. The following pages will show you not only how to perform each move, but will also give you an application of the technique to be used against an opponent.

FIST Breaking Techniques

In most cases, the hands are used to break things in a downward or straight-across motion. The feet almost always kick up to break. Two primary FIST breaking techniques are low breaking and straight or middle breaking.

Low breaking

(1) Take the ready stance slightly to the left of the object to be broken, your breaking fist nearly centered over the break point. (2) As your fist comes down, bring your body down with it. (3) Just before you break, pull back your nonbreaking fist, twisting your shoulders. This adds force to your breaking fist. (4) Hit the object at the middle of the end nearest you, using the force of the twisting motion and the full weight of your body. Remember to follow through. (5) A practical use for low fist breaking is a strike to the side of the neck when you are over your opponent.

APPLICATION

Middle breaking

(1) Use a standing ready stance. (2) Shift your weight to your rear foot while twisting your upper body. (3) Next, shift your weight to your forward foot while moving your body forward, building up power for your strike. (4) Continue your forward

motion with your body and (5) bring back your nonstriking fist as you hit your target and follow through.

(A) One application of this technique is a strike to the solar plexus.

A

KNIFE HAND
breaking techniques

Low breaking

(1) From a crouching ready position which centers your breaking hand over the block, (2) throw your upper body up, (3) twist it to build power and distance, (4) start the strike, bringing the body down through your original position, and (5) break the board at the middle of the end nearest you. Remember to keep the grain running vertical to your punch.

(A) A practical example of using this technique in a defensive situation is a strike to the back of the neck when your opponent tries to grab your legs.

1

4

5

2

3

A

Middle breaking

(1) Take a ready stance close to your target. (2) Make a soft practice strike to the exact spot you want to hit. (Important: do this even in a real defense situation. The accuracy gained is worth the time.) (3) Twist your body and bring your striking hand all the

way back. (4) Strike on a straight level and (5) strike with the grain.

(A) In practical self-defense, the knife-hand-middle-breaking technique can be applied as a strike under the ear.

A

RIDGEHAND
breaking techniques

Middle breaking

(1) Take a wide ready stance. (2) Bring back your striking hand, twisting your shoulders. (3) Put your body into your strike, twisting your shoulders back the other way and (4) bring your weight

forward along with it. (5) Break the board and follow through.

(A) A strike to the ribs is a practical application for this technique.

A

High breaking

(1) For high breaking with the ridgehand, take a ready position and (2) bring your striking arm back more on a downward angle (3) so that it can angle up as it strikes. (4) As you begin your strike, bring the striking arm up

through the neutral position at an upward angle. (5) Continue going up as you follow through.

(A) This technique can be used as a chin strike with ridgehand in a self-defense situation.

FINGERTIP
breaking techniques

Low breaking

(1) Take a ready stance. (2) Bring your elbow back and up. (3) Shift your weight forward and bring your hand down. (4) Strike through the target, keeping the direction of the grain in mind.

(A) When an opponent attempts a high kick, you can use this technique for a groin strike.

2

3

4

1

High breaking

(1) From the ready stance, (2) pull your elbow back, but not as high as for low breaking. (3) That way, your hand can go up further as you (4) strike your target and follow through.

(A) This technique can be employed in a strike to the eyes.

A

2

3

4

ELBOW STRIKE
breaking techniques

Low breaking

(1) From a crouching stance, with your elbow touching your target spot, (2) jump straight up. (3) When your feet first touch the ground, start to bring your arm down. (4) Bring your body down with your arm and (5) strike with your whole bodyweight behind the blow.

(A) When an opponent tries to grab your legs, you can use a low elbow strike to his spine.

1

4

5

2

3

A

High breaking

(1) From a ready stance, (2) twist your elbow and body to the right. (3) Bring your bodyweight forward with the strike and (4) break the target with the force of your whole body.

(A) A strike to the jaw is an example of this high breaking technique.

2

3

4

BACKFIST
breaking techniques

Middle breaking

(1) For the backfist, your ready stance begins with your fist already drawn back. (2) Whip it forward (3&4) with as much speed as you can and strike deeply.

(A) A strike to the cheek is an effective application of the backfist breaking technique.

2

3

4

JUMPING FRONT KICK
breaking technique

Middle breaking

(1) From a ready stance away from the target, (2) bring your rear foot forward while bending that knee. (3) Lift that knee up, then (4) jump and bring the other knee up higher than the first knee.

(5) As the first foot lands on the ground, break the target with the ball of your other foot.

(A) A jumping front kick is good for a kick to your opponent's stomach.

High breaking

(1) Again standing far back from your target, (2) bring your rear foot forward while bending the knee. (3) Jump higher with your other foot, and (4) as the first foot comes down while the other con-

tinues up (adding power), (5) break the board as you continue upward.

(A) In self-defense situations, a high jumping front kick can be used for a kick to the face.

1

FRONT KICK
breaking technique

Low breaking

(1) Standing away from the target, (2) bend the knee of your kicking foot and lift it. (3) Twist your body with the kick as it comes around and (4) *lift your heel* as you kick forward with the ball of your foot.

(A) To put this technique into action, use it for a kick to the groin. Remember, feet do their best job breaking things *upward.*

A

2

3

4

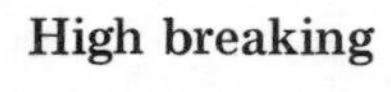

High breaking

(1) For higher kicking, (2) bend your knee, but do not lift it as high. (3) When your leg comes forward, (4) pull your knee up higher and (5) kick

4

5

your leg straight, breaking the target with your heel.

(A) This technique can be used for a front kick to the neck of an opponent.

A

ROUNDHOUSE KICK
breaking techniques

Middle breaking

(1) Looking at your target from a ready stance, (2) bring your knee up to the side, bending it, as you spin on the ball of your other foot. (3) Kick across the target and (4) break it with the ball of your foot.

(A) A middle roundhouse kick can be applied to your opponent's ribs.

2

3

4

1

High breaking

(1) Starting from the ready stance, (2) angle your knee up higher than for middle breaking and (3) bring it up higher when you spin. (4) Strike the target and follow through.

(A) A high roundhouse kick can be delivered to your opponent's face.

A

SIDE KICK
breaking technique

Middle breaking

(1) Starting in the ready position, (2) bring the rear knee forward and up. (3) Twist on the ball of your foot, (4) move your weight forward and bring your body along with it, then (5) kick to the mid-

dle of the end of the board with the heel of your foot.

(A) A middle side kick is effective on the middle of your opponent. The target is his stomach.

High breaking

(1) From the ready stance, (2) bring the rear knee up (3) higher than for middle breaking and (4) aim for the higher target. (5) As in middle breaking, your heel is up when you make impact.

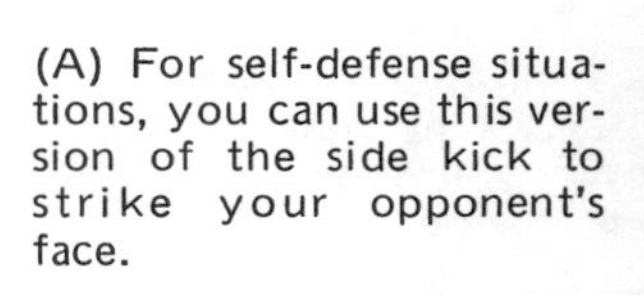

(A) For self-defense situations, you can use this version of the side kick to strike your opponent's face.

JUMPING SIDE KICK
breaking techniques

Middle breaking

(1) For the jumping side kick, take a ready stance with your rear knee bent slightly. (2) Bend both knees deeply in a squat and jump using both legs, moving forward with the jump. (3) As you fly toward your target, bring your right foot up higher and (4) break the board with a ridgefoot.

(A) Like the middle roundhouse kick, your target for a middle jumping side kick can be your opponent's ribs.

2

3

4

High breaking

(1) From the same stance as for middle breaking, (2) crouch with both legs and (3) jump—higher than for middle breaking, but with the right knee more level with the left knee. (4)

Then the right foot comes up higher and (5) the strike is made.

(A) In a self-defense situation, this technique can be used for a kick to the face.

A

SPINNING BACK KICK
breaking techniques

Left forward stance

(1) When your target is near, start with your left foot forward for your spinning back kick. (2) Bend your left knee and spin your right leg backwards in the direction of the arrow. (3) Jump with your left foot and (4) break the board with the ridge of your right foot.

(A) Both left and right forward stances can be used for a middle kick to the stomach . . . .

A

2
PUGILI

3

4

Right forward stance

(1) When your target is further away, begin with your right foot forward in the ready stance. First, swing your left foot forward, spinning on your right foot, then in the same fluid movement, (2) spin on your left foot, bringing your right foot around backward as you

did for your left forward stance spinning back kick. (3) The rest of the kick is executed just like the left stance, (4) bringing your right foot around to (5) strike the target with a ridgefoot.

(A) . . . or to the face.

A

HOOK KICK
breaking techniques

Right forward stance

(1) When you close in on your target, use a right forward stance for your hook kick. Start with your left knee slightly bent. (2) Raise up your right knee and (3) kick so that your heel goes to the side of your target, then (4) down

and through the target, all in one fluid movement. (5) Remember to follow through.

(A) The hook kick, right or left forward stance, is good for a kick to the head . . . .

Left forward stance

(1) For a target further away, start in the left forward stance. (2) Bring your right foot up and forward, (3) start the forward part of your kick, (4) snap it

up to the side of your target and (5) break it as you come down with your heel.

(A) . . . or to the face.

A

SPIN KICK
breaking techniques

Without hook

(1) Take a ready stance close to your target. (2) Lift your rear leg up and spin backward. (3) Continue your spin and straighten your leg. (4) Kick in an arc with your knee straight.

(A) Whether your opponent is close in . . . .

2

3

4

With hook

(1) Starting further away from your target, (2) spin backward with your rear leg up. (3) But unlike the spin kick without hook, continue spinning with your knee bent and (4) kick with your knee bent. Remember to lift your heel as you kick, for more power.

(A) . . . or further away, the target in a self-defense situation can be your opponent's face.

2

3

4

Left forward stance

(1) For a close opponent, start with your left foot forward. (2) Jump straight up with a turning motion and (3) as you continue to spin, bend both knees, with the right going higher. (4) Start the kick and (5) break the target with a

ridgefoot, bringing your right arm down for more power and balance.

(A) The jumping spin kick can strike the face of your opponent in an aggressive defense maneuver or . . . .

Right forward stance

(1) Start on your right foot forward when an opponent is further away. (2) Take a step forward before you (3) jump and spin, (4) coming around with a ridgefoot to (5) break the

target. Follow through, and then get ready for a landing.

(A) . . . as a counter to his offensive.

A

Chapter 9

CONTROL KICKING

You can have all the speed, power and penetration of a grand master, but it will do you little good without control. It is important to always strike accurately, hitting the exact spot necessary to break your target. So keep up your concentration for every kick, every punch, and practice the exercise in this chapter as often as possible.

Small target

For correct breaking techniques, it is important to have these abilities: speed, power, tough striking areas and—control. Using a small item like a cigarette for a target forces you to develop the ability to hit a specific spot.

(1) With an assistant kindly allowing a cigarette to be placed in his right ear,

take a slightly crouching ready stance back and to his right. Start spinning your right foot around backward, and (2) as you jump, bend your right knee. (3) Continue your spin and begin your kick with the ball of your foot. (4) Follow through—kicking as hard as if you were breaking a board—(5) and land on your left foot.

Two feet split kick

Another way to practice control is to break two targets at the same time. This not only requires that you hit the correct spot, but coordinate your body to use both feet effectively.

(1) Start with your right foot forward. To get off the ground, bring left foot forward, and (2) kick down with your left foot.

(3) As your right foot leaves the ground, bend the right knee. (4) Your left foot comes off the ground as your right knee continues up. (5) As you approach your high point, both knees are bent. (6) Kick out both feet at the same time, breaking the boards with the balls of your feet. (7) Land on both feet at the same time.

Jumping breaking kick over a barrier

Not only does this technique build the control and coordination which is the goal of such exercises, it has an exotic practical application. Here the barrier is a wall of students. In a self-defense situation, the barrier could be anything, including a ring of assailants.

(1) Get in a ready position far away from the barrier, the left foot back for a fast take-off to gain speed.

(2) As you kick off with your left foot, throw the right leg forward and up. (3) As the left foot comes up to join the right, both knees almost touch your chest. (4) Keep this position as you fly over the barrier. (5) As you approach your target, snap out with your right foot and break the board with a ridgefoot. (6) Your kicking foot should still be outstretched as you touch earth with your left foot.

Breaking two targets while in air

In practicing this technique, you build up a great deal of speed as well as accuracy. You must learn to make two kicks at different targets accurately and with enough power behind each kick to break the target. In a self-defense situation against two or more opponents, this technique is very valuable.

(1) Take a standard ready stance away from the targets. (2) Bend both knees. (3) Kick off the ground with your right foot and bend your left leg upward

as you start to spin to your right. (4) Get your left foot ready to kick the target while the right foot is leaving the ground and starting to follow the left foot. (5) Execute a spinning side kick to the target on the right-hand with the ball of your left foot. (6) While still spinning in the air, break the target on the left with a back kick with the heel of your right foot. (7) Make a landing to the right of the broken targets, with your back to them but still looking at them.

1

2

3

Three-target breaking

For advanced practice, the next step is three-target breaking.

(1) Starting a little closer to the targets, kick off with your left foot and bring your right foot up. (2) Bring your right knee up to your chest while the left foot comes up. (3) Fly

to the first target. (4) Break the far right target with your left foot, using a ridgefoot side kick. (5) Come around with a roundhouse kick and break the center target with the ball of your right foot. (6) Just before landing, smash the left-hand target with your right fist.

Low-high hook kick

Another example of two-target breaking is the low-high hook kick. Its practical use is for two targets on the same opponent, one low (like the knee) and one high (like the face).

(1) From the ready stance, start to move your forward foot upward (2)

while your rear foot slides backward. (3) Kick to the bottom target with a heel (hook) kick and (4) follow through, then (5) hook upward and break high target with a second hook. Remember to keep the heel of your standing foot off the ground when you make contact.

1

2

Spinning low-high kick

A third version of two-target breaking is the spinning low-high kick.

(1) After you take a ready stance, spin on the ball of your left foot. (2) As you spin, bring up your right foot. (3) Break the low

target with the heel of your right foot and (4) follow through. (5) Still spinning, hook your right foot up to the high target and break it with your heel. Always remember to hit the board with the grain and follow through.

Chapter 10

SPARRING

Always try to meet an offensive move with a *counteroffensive* move, not just a block. How do you turn your opponent's offense to your advantage and make it into *your* offense? One example is countering a lunge punch to the face with a hook (heel) kick.

High hook kick

(1) You both start with your weight on both feet in identical ready stances. (2) Your opponent takes the offensive by shifting his weight forward, the start of a lunge punch. You raise your forward knee. (3) As your opponent lunges forward, you tilt your body back and continue to bring your knee up. (4) When your

opponent is ready to punch, your foot is right beside his head. (5) Your foot comes straight across at his head, parallel to the ground, and you end the encounter with a heel to the face.

(A) For more power, you can practice this move as a breaking technique, using a board for the target.

SUMMARY

The serious practitioner of the martial arts will have learned from this book that weight, speed, focus, penetration and concentration are essential cornerstones to the mastery of breaking techniques. To use them effectively, they must be coordinated into a working unit. Your body thus becomes an efficient, deadly machine. To accomplish this goal, you must be in the best physical condition. You must have flexibility. Work on one element at a time. Start with focus, add concentration, then penetration. Put your weight into what you're doing. When your accuracy is carefully developed, add speed.

The key to success in breaking techniques is similar to any other of the arts—practice. To practice well requires dedication. With all of these elements going for you, you should have developed a well-coordinated technique. Use it to keep in shape. Use it

Pu Gill Gwon

Acknowledgements

This book is dedicated to martial artists all over the world. For years, ever since I was with the Korean Naval Intelligence Service, I have wanted to share my tae kwon do in written form. Now, with the kind assistance of Ohara Publications and their staff, one part of the knowledge which has been imparted to me is available to you. Special thanks to Han Kim, Publisher of Ohara Publications; to Geri Simon, who did the outstanding graphic design for this volume; to Ed Ikuta, for his excellent photography; and to Nick O'Prancter, for his valuable assistance in the writing process.